SAN DIEGO

Text by
JOHN W. GILBERT

Photos by
ANDREA PISTOLESI

ŦB
BONECHI

INDEX

© Copyright by CASA EDITRICE BONECHI
Via Cairoli, 18/b Firenze - Italia - Tel.+39 055576841 - Fax +39 0555000766
E-mail: bonechi@bonechi.it - Internet: www.bonechi.it

Printed in Italy by Centro Stampa Editoriale Bonechi

Text by John W. Gilbert.

NEW YORK ADDRESS:
98 Thompson Street # 38 - New York, N.Y. 10012
Ph: (212) 343-9235 - Fax: (212) 625-9636
e-mail: bonechinyc@aol.com

The photographs taken by ANDREA PISTOLESI
are the property of the Publisher's archives.
The reproduction of the photographs on pages 40-43 and 57-59 is a courtesy of San Diego Zoo *and* San Diego Sea World.
Photographs on page 62: The Flower Fields® at Carlsbad Ranch - Carlsbad, California
Photographs on page 63: LEGOLAND® California

ISBN 88-476-0528-8

* * *

*California's first Spanish Mission: The **Mission San Diego de Alcala**.*

HISTORICAL INTRODUCTION

For ten thousand years the coast of Southern
California was home to various tribes of Native
American Indians who prospered off the
abundant resources of sea and land. The warm sunny
climate favored the Indians' lifestyles based on fishing
and hunting, in harmony with the natural world. But with
the arrival of European explorers in the Sixteenth and
Seventeenth Centuries, and finally settlers in the
Eighteenth, the brutal process of European conquest
and colonization was set into motion which in a
relatively short time would lead to the destruction of the
Native American societies then existing in Southern
California.

The Spanish conquistador Hernando Cortés gave the
area the name of California, after exploring what is
today the Mexican peninsula of Baja California in 1538.
Incredibly, Cortés had believed it to be the island-
home of the legendary Queen Calafia whose kingdom
of black women warriors was much sought-after "for,
on the whole island, there was no metal but gold."
The first European to actually explore the coast of

present-day California was the Portugese explorer Juan
Rodriguez Cabrillo. Sailing under the Spanish flag,
through "great storms of rain, heavy clouds, great
darkness, and heavy air," Cabrillo landed at what is
today Point Loma in the San Diego harbor on
September 28, 1542. The explorer's two Spanish
caravels, the San Salvador and the Victoria, sat out a
storm for nearly a week in the "enclosed and very
good" natural harbor which he gave the name of San
Miguel. Cabrillo's party was met by the region's
indigenous inhabitants, a people related to the Yuma
Indians called the Kumeyaay, who Cabrillo described
as "comely and large." But despite the fact that the area
was already populated, Cabrillo followed the usual
colonial practice of claiming the territory for the Spanish
King before his ships set off again, continuing up the
coast as far north as present-day Oregon.

The next Spanish explorer to visit the area was
Sebastian Vizcaino in 1602. He promptly renamed the
harbor San Diego for the patron of his expedition, St.
James of Alcala. Despite Vizcaino's enthusiatic accounts

of the beauty and natural resources he found along the California coast, another 167 years were to pass before another group of explorers returned to San Diego.

In 1769, worried about the presence of Russian seal-pelt traders who had been pushing steadily south along the Pacific coast, the Spanish King Carlos III ordered a military expedition to the area. Three Spanish caravels led by Captain Gaspar de Potola and accompanied by the Franciscan missionary Padre Junipero Serra were sent from Mexico with instructions to establish a string of forts and mission settlements along the coast. One of the ships was lost at sea, but the other two arrived in San Diego harbor in the spring of 1769.

On July 16, 1769 Potola's soldiers and Padre Serra's Franciscans established the first Catholic mission and presidio (fort) in California on a high hill inland from the harbor in what today is San Diego's "Old Town" quarter. Only the barest of ruins remain to mark the spot of the 1769 Spanish presidio.

The mission was moved six miles inland in 1774 to Mission Valley along the San Diego River where the Mission Basilica San Diego de Alcala still stands today. Padre Serra, known as "the Apostle of California," went on to establish a string of nine missions which by 1823 had grown in number to 21, each a day's journey apart, spread along El Camino Real, or "the royal highway," stretching north along the coast. These missions, virtually self-sufficient economic enterprises dependent on the exploitation of Native American labor, were to be instrumental in fulfilling the Spanish colonial project in California.

When Mexico won its independence from Spain in 1821, California became a Mexican territory. The Spanish forts, missions and settlements in California thus passed under Mexican rule. The Franciscan missionaries refused their allegiance to the new revolutionary government in Mexico City and returned to Spain. The missions were then secularized by the Mexican government and 8 million acres of land were divided up into roughly 800 private ranches and handed out to the Spanish-Mexican "Californios." The San Diego mission was turned over to Santiago Arguello.

In the meantime, the United States government on the east coast of North America had begun to take an interest in the vast tracts of Mexican land in the American southwest, including California. Yankee ships had been increasing their trade with the Mexican cattle ranchers along the California coast. And by 1845, about 500 American settlers were living in California. That same year U.S. President James Polk took office with the firm intention of taking possession of California, along with other territories, away from Mexico.

In 1846 the U.S. proceeded to provoke a war with Mexico along the Rio Grande River in what is now Texas. Shortly before, a contingent of U.S. soldiers under the command of John Frémont, together with a group of U.S. settlers, had proclaimed the independent "Bear Flag Republic" at Sonoma in Northern California.

With the outbreak of war, U.S. forces landed and together with Frémont's men drove the Mexicans out of Southern California. Despite tough resistance from Mexican settlers near San Diego, the U.S. had taken complete possession of California by early 1847. It became an official U.S. territory with the Treaty of Guadalupe Hidalgo in 1848.

In that same year, gold was discovered in California's Sacramento Valley. The ensuing gold rush led to a massive influx of fortune seekers, the so-called "forty-niners," who dramatically increased the population and transformed the face of the territory. Despite the opposition of the Southern slave states, California was admitted as the thirty-first state of the Union in 1850 with a state constitution prohibiting the institution of slavery. Also in 1850, San Diego was incorporated as a city and became the name of California's first county.

In 1867, Alonzo Erastus Horton arrived in San Diego. He proceeded to fix municipal elections, and then bought some 1,000 acres of prime waterfront real estate on the harbor at a mere 21 cents an acre. This area was given the name of "New Town", and Horton began to sell or give away plots of land to encourage the city center's move west from "Old Town." Much of Old Town was burned down in a fire in 1872, further accelerating the growth of New Town. Its fine natural harbor, one of the best in North America and indeed in the world, had already turned San Diego into a busy port. In 1885 there followed a boom in urban development and population growth in San Diego with the arrival of the transcontinental Santa Fe Railroad. Immigration to Southern California soared as the railroad lines facilitated travel as well as the development of agriculture. Irrigation of Southern California's arid, semi-desert lands permitted the planting of vast citrus orchards as well as other important cash crops, making agriculture a major national industry.

The discovery of oil near Los Angeles in 1892 laid the foundation for the industrial boom which was to characterize Southern Californian economic expansion in the Twentieth Century. And with the Panama-California Exposition in 1915, international attention was drawn to the commercial potential of San Diego's harbor.

The Great Depression of 1929 was followed by another wave of immigration. Adding to the influx were several hundred thousand farmers and their families who left Oklahoma, Missouri, Arkansas and Northern Texas to find new homes in Southern California as a terrible drought beginning in 1930 turned an area stretching from Texas to the Dakotas into a giant "dust bowl." Immigration from Mexico had also continued through the years at a steady rate.

In the Twentieth Century, California, and San Diego in particular, increasingly assumed strategic military importance, in particular during World War II, and the Korean and Vietnamese Wars, as it was transformed into a logistical base for the U.S. military in the Pacific. San Diego County became the home of the U.S. Navy's 11th Naval District, the Marine Corps' Camp Pendleton, as well as major aeronautical and other military-related industries. By 1963 California had become the most populated state in the U.S.

There are over 26 million people living in the state today. And among the 16 million people currently living in Southern California are to be found people of all races and ethnic backgrounds — a true melting pot of cultures and lifestyles!

*A striking panorama of the **San Diego** skyline and harbor with the majestic mountains of the Cleveland National Forest in the distance.*

SAN DIEGO

San Diego in the extreme southwest near the Mexican border was historically the first crossroads in Spanish California, and represents the actual birthplace of the Golden State. Today the city is the sixth largest in the U.S. and California's second largest after Los Angeles, with a population of over a million. But despite its relative size, San Diego has maintained a distinctly smalltown charm. More than a single, concentrated urban center, the city seems like a collection of smaller communities: Old Town, Coronado, Point Loma, Mission Beach and La Jolla to name a few.

San Diego County, with a population of some two and a half million, is the seventh largest in the U.S.A. Its striking natural landscapes represent all the geographical diversity of Southern California, with ocean beaches, mountain forests and arid desert all within an easy day's ride of each other. There are over sixty golf courses in the county, as well as quite a number of State Parks and the Cleveland National Forest. Over seventy miles of Pacific coast make the county a paradise for water sports and boating. And the two and a half hour drive to Los Angeles from San Diego (125 miles), is a delightful excursion, as is the beautiful train ride.

In and around San Diego, as in the rest of Southern California, a car facilitates getting around greatly. A network of freeways connects the beaches with downtown and other inland communities. But unfortunately San Diego is not immune to Southern California's traffic congestion and its infamous drivers. The city's excellent trolley system, however, offers an alternative to both cars and the other less convenient forms of public transport.

San Diego itself is a rather relaxed, very liveable city. The climate is stupendous: sunny, warm and dry with an average year-round temperature of 70 degrees Fahrenheit. Tropical gardens and landscaping surround the homes and public buildings. There is an impressive and expanding skyline, and the arts and culture are flourishing.

The city has earned itself the nickname "Sportstown, U.S.A." with all that it offers the amateur sportsman, as well as its many professional sports teams. The 60,000-seat Jack Murphy Stadium is home to the San Diego Padres baseball team, the Chargers (football), and the Sockers (soccer).

The city was the site of the America's Cup sailing competition in 1992 with the San Diego Yacht Club as the Cup Defender. All these factors, along with San Diego's acclaimed beaches, make the city one of America's great vacation capitals. In fact tourism is now the city's third largest industry, after manufacturing and the military.

Boats docked along San Diego's downtown waterfront, across North Harbor Drive from the **San Diego County Administration Building.**

Stately palms along a street in San Diego's downtown district.

On the following page:
The **Maritime Museum's** iron windjammer **"The Star of India",** brilliantly lit at sunset on the San Diego Harbor.

THE SAN DIEGO HARBOR

San Diego's excellent natural harbor, one of the finest in the world, had made the city a bustling port town in the 1800s when Yankee trader ships began arriving to exchange their manufactured wares with the Spanish-Mexican "rancheros" for cow hides and tallow.

The city's lucrative fishing industry was initiated in the 1800s by Chinese immigrants in their junks along the shores of Point Loma. It was subsequently taken over by Italian fishermen, and then the Portuguese whose community has been an important part of the city since the 1880s.

The city dredged the harbor to deepen it in 1927. And later, after the city had become an important U.S. Naval base, the harbor was again dredged at the time of World War II to allow greater access for Navy ships. **Harbor** and **Shelter Islands**, resort peninsulas connected to the mainland, were man-made with the tons of rock and sludge dredged from the harbor bottom.

Yacht clubs, fish markets, restaurants, and hotels crowd the waterfront. All types of seacraft fill the harbor waters, from houseboats and fishing boats to cruise ships and naval vessels.

Seagulls fly overhead as seals swim among the boats. The waterfront downtown has seen particular development with the construction of Seaport Village, the Embarcadero and the new Convention Center. Tour boats and whale-watching ships leave from the harbor to visit the bay and points along the coast.

The **Embarcadero** is a delightful walkway along the harbor which stretches a mile or so from the B Street and Broadway Piers in the north, south to the

Some of the innovative new architecture illuminating San Diego's expanding skyline at dusk.

A view of the San Diego Harbor and skyline.

Embarcadero Marina Park in Seaport Village. The Embarcadero pathway follows the waterfront along Harbor Drive past restaurants, piers with cruise ships and tour boats, naval vessels of the Eleventh Naval District, fish markets, hotels and shops. It is a popular place for jogging, bicycling, or merely strolling along and taking in all the sights the harbor has to offer.

The **San Diego Maritime Museum** is another leading attraction in the harbor. It consists of three ships, fully restored, which are docked at the Embarcadero.

The most spectacular of the museum's ships is without doubt the **"Star of India."** An iron windjammer built on the Isle of Man and first launched in 1863, the "Star of India" made some 27 voyages around the world in its day. The ship was retired from active service in 1926 and restoration was begun in 1959. Now this iron merchant ship is the oldest vessel of its kind still afloat.

The two other Maritime Museum ships include the 1898 **"Berkeley,"** a beautifully decorated paddle-wheel ferryboat, and the 1904 iron-hulled steam yacht **"Medea."**

The blue, yellow, and white-tiled domes of downtown's **Santa Fe Depot.**

A busy street in downtown San Diego.

DOWNTOWN SAN DIEGO

San Diego's downtown district is located some three miles southeast of the International Airport, directly south of Balboa Park, and across the harbor from Coronado. The area has undergone an extensive and extremely ambitious redevelopment program over the last two decades, transforming not only the city's skyline, but the very character of the city's commercial center as well. The downtown waterfront along Harbor Drive and its main artery Broadway, in particular, have witnessed a boom in new construction.

The **San Diego County Administration Building** north of Broadway on North Harbor Drive, facing the harbor, is well worth a visit. Built in the Spanish-Colonial style in 1938 as part of a Depression-era public works project, the 10-story tower is quite impressive when illuminated at night. There is a cafeteria on the tenth floor serving relatively inexpensive food and affording spectacular views of the harbor and downtown.

South of the County Administration Building and two blocks from the waterfront, but still north of

Broadway, is the **Santa Fe Depot.** The present structure was constructed in 1915 in preparation for the Panama-California Exposition. It replaced an earlier train depot which had been built in 1887. The Santa Fe Depot was restored in 1983, and is now a registered historical site. Its Spanish-Colonial style is highlighted by blue, yellow and white-tiled twin domes similar to the tile work on the California Tower in Balboa Park.

San Diego's superb **trolley system** connects the Santa Fe Depot with some 17 other stations inland north and east, and south to the Mexican border. The bright red trolleys are both highly efficient and inexpensive. The Bayfront Line connects downtown with Seaport Village, the Convention Center, and the waterfront hotels. It is only a twenty-minute trolley ride south to the San Ysidro-Tijuana border, the busiest international border in the world with some thirty million crossing annually.

The historic **Gaslamp Quarter** is south of Broadway along 5th Avenue. It occupies a 38-acre, 16-square block area in the heart of what was once Horton's "New Town." For years a rather seedy, crime-ridden district of bars, porn shops and flop houses,

*Downtown's **Horton Plaza**: a shopping, dining and entertainment extravaganza!*

the quarter has been transformed through an ambitious renovation project begun in the 1970s. The original Victorian buildings from the late 1800s have been restored, and the area is now a National Historic District. The tree-lined streets have brick-paved sidewalks, wrought-iron benches and gaslamp-style street lights. There are many fine restaurants, clubs and shops. A walk along 5th Avenue and adjoining streets is well worth the time.

Of particular note are the William Heath Davis House (1850), housing the Gaslamp Quarter Association and providing information and tours, the Horton Grand Hotel (1888), complete with a ghost haunting room 309, the Stingaree Building, the Backesto Building, the twin towers of the Louis Bank of Commerce, the Keating Building, the Mercantile Building, the Villa Montezuma, and the Jewelers' Exchange Building.

One of the most spectacular additions to San Diego's downtown in the last decade has without doubt been the new **Horton Plaza** adjoining the Gaslamp Quarter. Built in 1985 in the heart of the old downtown district, around the original park and fountain of the old Horton Plaza on Broadway, this immense 6-floor shopping, dining and entertainment mall covers some 9.5 acres — more than six city blocks! The pastel-colored expanse is a virtual labyrinth decorated with colorful tilework, arches, cupolas, sculptures, and banners. There are three major department stores, over 150 smaller shops, all kinds of restaurants, a deluxe hotel, art galleries and movie theaters. It also has its own parking facilities. From the top floor restaurants there are great panoramas of downtown, the harbor and Balboa Park. Plan on spending several mornings or afternoons to get a real idea of all that Horton Plaza has to offer!

*An aerial view of downtown's **Seaport Village.***

*Sunset at the **Harbor House** restaurant, serving seafood on the waterfront in **Seaport Village.***

On the following pages:
Boutiques and restaurants in the exquisitely-landscaped
Seaport Village.

At the southern end of the Embarcadero waterfront walkway is another major addition to San Diego's downtown, **Seaport Village.** Built in 1980 on 23 acres of prime waterfront on the site of the old Coronado Ferry Landing, Seaport Village has been instrumental in rejuvenating downtown San Diego. The beautifully-landscaped village consists of a great variety of boutiques and restaurants housed in stucco and clapboard buildings combining traditional Spanish-Colonial, Victorian and Old Monterey architectural styles.

The village's chief landmark is its 45-foot replica of the Mukiteo Lighthouse in Everett, Washington. The structure houses the San Diego Pier Café. Another attraction is the Broadway Flying Horses Carousel, constructed in 1890 with handcarved animals, and transplanted from its original site in Coney Island, New York. There is also a city park on a grassy fishing pier jutting out into the bay, ideal for fishing, picnics, kite-flying or whatever. Seaport Village's many restaurants offer splendid views of San Diego's bustling harbor.

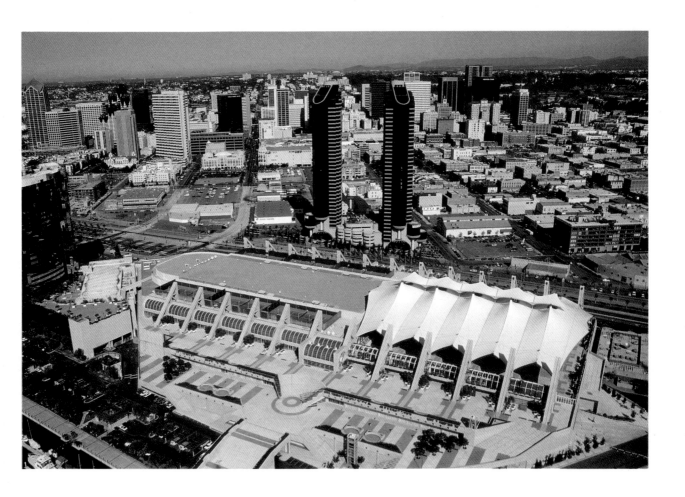

On pages 20-21:
Sunset over San Diego Harbor as seen from the southern end of the **Embarcadero** *waterfront walkway in* **Seaport Village.**

San Diego's downtown skyline with the 25-story twin mirrored towers of the luxurious 1,355-room San Diego **Marriott Hotel and Marina** *south of Seaport Village on the waterfront. The San Diego* **Convention Center** *is at the end of the marina on the far-right.*

An aerial view of San Diego's enormous new **Convention Center.**

South of Seaport Village on Harbor Drive is the latest addition to the downtown waterfront, the new **San Diego Convention Center.** In operation since 1990, the Convention Center was constructed at a cost of some $160 million and occupies 760,000 square feet. Its distinctive architecture is truly striking! The 100,000 square-foot top deck has no roof, but is instead covered with white, teflon-covered sails. The overall effect is that of an enormous sailing ship or winged creature rising up from the bay. The Convention Center has frequent trade shows open to the public, and it is possible to tour the building.

The surrounding area has hotels in all price ranges. The luxurious 25-story, mirrored-glass twin towers of the 1,355-room San Diego Marriott Hotel and Marina built in 1983 rise above the waterfront north of the Convention Center.

*Three views of the **Casa del Prado** in **Balboa Park**.*

BALBOA PARK

San Diego's urban jewel is without a doubt the stupendous **Balboa Park** sprawling over 1,400 acres of canyons and hillsides north of the downtown area. The parkland was set aside by far-seeing city fathers in 1868, and was then left for decades in its original wild, natural state.

In 1915 the park was chosen as the site of the city's Panama-California Exposition in celebration of the completion of the Panama Canal. The intention of city leaders was to attract international attention to San Diego as a world-class commercial and industrial center. The Exposition Committee made extensive plans to refurbish the city's infrastructure and adorn Balboa Park with stately Spanish-Colonial style buildings, with colonnades and tiled roofs, to house the Exposition. Decorative fountains and patios were constructed, and ornamental shrubs and trees from all over the world were planted to landscape the park. The Exposition was a smashing success and the new architecture became a permanent addition to the park's topography. More buildings were added with the California Pacific Exposition of 1935-36.

Renowned for its scenic beauty and romantic architecture, Balboa Park was a much sought-after site for shooting films in the early years of cinema. Among the many films with scenes shot in the park, of special note are Fatty Arbuckles' "Fatty at San Diego" in 1913, Mack Sennett's "Fatty and Mabel at the San Diego Exposition" with comedians Fatty Arbuckle and Mabel Normand in 1915, Allan Dwan's "Soldiers of Fortune" in 1919, "The Dictator" starring Wallace Reid in 1922, Orson Welles' 1942 classic "Citizen Kane," and Mickey Rooney in "The Fireball" in 1950.

The balustraded **Cabrillo Bridge** was built in 1914 as the gateway to the park and official entrance to the

1915 Exposition. It spans what was formerly the Laguna Cabrillo and is now the Cabrillo Freeway at the western end of the park. There is a wonderful view from the bridge. During the Christmas season, the park is strung with colorful lights and makes an enchanting sight. It is the only cantilevered bridge in California.

The main artery of Balboa Park is **El Prado,** a museum-lined avenue stretching from the Cabrillo Bridge at the park's entrance, past the Museum of Art where it becomes a pedestrian mall, and then on till it reaches the 60-foot fountain in Balboa Plaza. The city's finest museums are here, as well as theaters and meeting rooms.

A close-up of the facade and colorful tiled dome of the **Museum of Man.**

The Museum of Man's magnificent 200-foot **California Tower.**

The **Museum of Man** is situated at the official entrance to the park in the former California Building. This striking quadrangle around a central plaza is one of the few original Spanish-Colonial style buildings in the park. The structure was renovated in the late 1980s. Across California Plaza is the 1915 Spanish-Colonial style **Chapel of St. Francis.**

Towering over the Museum of Man is the 200-foot Spanish-Colonial style **California Tower** with its blue and white-tiled dome. Its magnificent 100-bell carillon, chimes every quarter hour. The tower's base features life-size sculptured figures from California's history, including Padre Junipero Serra, Sebastian Vizcaino, and Padre Luis Jayme.

The museum was established in 1915 to show "the story of man through the ages." It now displays exhibitions of various Native American cultures from across the Americas, including the area's indigenous Kumeyaay Indians.

There are also live craft demonstrations. The museum has a plaster cast of an erect, walking human ancestor named "Lucy," the oldest skeleton in the world of its kind. With 67,000 items in its permanent collection, the Museum of Man is considered one of the finest anthropological museums in the U.S.

Next door to the Museum of Man, under the California Tower, is the **Simon Edison Center for the Performing Arts.** This theatrical complex includes the **Old Globe Theatre,** the **Cassius Carter Center Stage,** and an outdoor **Festival Stage** for summer theatrical productions. The original 1915 Old Globe Theater was destroyed by fire in 1978. It was rebuilt and then reopened in 1982. The theater is a faithful replica of Shakespeare's original Globe Theatre on the Thames.
The theatrical company's accomplished repertoire of Shakespeare's works as well as other productions has earned it a solid reputation over the years.

*Two views of the **Museum of Art's** 16th-century Spanish-Renaissance style facade, with life-size statues of the Spanish painters Velazquez, Murillo and Zurbaran, and the coats-of-arms of San Diego, California, the U.S.A. and Spain.*
The seashell over the doorway represents the giant shell said to have carried St. James to Spain.

Continuing east along El Prado, one comes to a building with an extremely ornate 16th-century Spanish-Renaissance style facade housing the **San Diego Museum of Art.** The facade bears life-size statues of the Spanish painters Murillo, Zurbaran and Velazquez, as well as the coats of arms of San Diego, California, the U.S. and Spain.

Established in 1924-26, the museum is now home to one of the best art collections on the West Coast. Spanish Baroque, Italian Renaissance, Flemish, and Dutch painting is represented in the works of such masters as Velazquez, Goya, El Greco, Titian, Giorgione, Tintoretto, Rubens, Rembrandt and Van Dyke. There is also a **Sculpture Garden** with some twenty works by Henry Moore, Marino Marini and Francisco Zuniga. The museum is noted for its special, and often controversial, exhibitions. Next door to the Art Museum is the delightful

Timken Gallery. Established in 1965, this private gallery is home to a small collection of European masterpieces dating from the Fourteenth to the Twentieth Centuries and including works by Rembrandt, Rubens, Pisarro and Cézanne. There are American works from the Nineteenth Century, and the museum also has a fine collection of Russian icons.

Parking facilities are found in Balboa Park's largest square, the central **Plaza de Panama.** Situated south of the Museum of Art and half-way between the Cabrillo Bridge and the Plaza de Balboa, the Plaza de Panama was constructed for the 1915 Exposition. In 1927 **El Cid**, a 23-foot-tall sculpture by Anna Hyatt Huntington, was erected in the plaza. The statue commemorates Campeador Rodrigo Diaz de Bivar (known as Cid) who drove the Moors out of Spain in the Eleventh Century.

*Balboa Park's redwood open-air **Botanical Building** and 275-foot-long **Lily Pond.***

At the southern end of the plaza is the **Spreckles Outdoor Organ Pavilion** with its gigantic 5,000 pipe organ. Donated for the 1915 Exposition, it is the largest outdoor organ in the world. There are free afternoon concerts on Sundays. The organ's melodious sounds drifting through the air make up an essential part of the park's characteristic atmosphere.

East of the Plaza de Panama, El Prado becomes a pedestrian mall. Stop at the **House of Hospitality** (1915) to visit the Balboa Park Information Center for maps, brochures, guide books or other information, as well as for souvenirs and postcards.
Be sure to see the tile fountain in the building's courtyard with its beautiful statue of a Mexican girl pouring water from a jar.

Sculptor Donal Hord carved the statue from a 1,200 pound block of limestone for the 1935 Exposition. Across El Prado from the House of Hospitality is the **Botanical Building.** Built for the 1915 Exposition, it is a huge, 250-foot-long, open-air building of redwood lathing with free entrance. Inside there are over 500 varieties of tropical and subtropical plants, with waterfalls, fountains, and a magnificent orchid collection.

In front of the Botanical Building stretches the 275 foot-long **Laguna de las Flores,** also known as the **Lily Pond.** During World War II the pond was used as a swimming pool by the military.
Today the pond is filled with giant koi fish, and its colorful water lilies and lotuses provide the background for musicians, mimes, magicians and

*Two views of the **Casa del Prado Theater**.*   *The entrance to San Diego's **Natural History Museum**.*

other street artists who perform along the pond's lawns, especially on weekends.
 It is a favorite spot for taking photos and sunbathing.

Next to the Botanical Building and the Lily Pond is the **Casa del Prado** with its beautifully adorned facade. After the 1968 earthquake, the original 1914-15 building was sold to a wrecking company and torn down. Much of the original statuary was preserved, and then incorporated in the new Spanish-Colonial style building which opened in 1971. The building contains the **Casa del Prado Theater.**

After the Casa del Prado is the **Natural History Museum,** the last building on the El Prado before arriving in the Plaza de Balboa. Originally founded in

1874, the museum has been housed in the present low building since 1933. Its exhibitions deal predominantly with local geology and minerals, ocean ecology, and animal life, including endangered and extinct species. Of special interest are the dinosaur bones, the seismograph and the Foucault pendulum. The museum also has an 88,000 volume library. There are interesting hands-on exhibits for children. The museum is often home to visiting shows as well. Among the museum's most popular attractions are the whale-watching trips it organizes, and its tours of the park's canyons and hillsides.

Across the Plaza de Balboa from the Natural History Museum lies the **Reuben H. Fleet Space Theater**

*Two views of San Diego's **Hall of Champions** in the **Casa de Balboa**, commemorating local sports history.*

*San Diego's modernistic **Aerospace Historical Center**, home to the **San Diego Aerospace Museum** and the International Aerospace Hall of Fame.*

and Science Center, established in 1973. Behind its Spanish-Colonial style facade is the largest planetarium in the U.S., a laserium, and the first Omnimax theater in the world with a 75-foot dome and overhead screen. Throughout the day films are shown on the history of the universe, space, and the natural world. The Science Center has fascinating educational exhibits for both children and adults.

Heading back west along El Prado, one comes to the **Casa de Balboa,** across the street from the Casa del Prado. The original 1914 building was destroyed by arson in 1978, but then reconstructed as faithfully as

possible in 1980. It currently serves as home to four museums: the **Museum of San Diego History,** the **Model Railroad Museum,** the **Museum of Photographic Arts,** and the **San Diego Hall of Champions.**

Nicknamed "Sportstown, U.S.A.," San Diego has an impressive local sports history which is commemorated with a vast amount of memorabilia in its **Hall of Champions.** All of the city's hometown greats receive recognition here, including baseball's Don Larsen, 400 hitter Ted Williams, basketball's Bill Walton, America's Cup champion Dennis Conner,

*Hands-on educational exhibitions at the **Reuben H. Fleet Space Theater & Science Center**.*

*Two views of the original and replica aircraft on display at the **San Diego Aerospace Museum**, including a replica of Charles Lindbergh's "Spirit of St. Louis."*

Florence Chadwick, the first woman to swim the English Channel both ways, Archie Moore, light-heavyweight title holder in boxing, U.S. Open Golf champions Gene Littler and Billy Casper, and Wimbledon champions Maureen Connolly and Karen Hantze, to name but a few.

Leaving El Prado and heading southeast to the Pan American Plaza, one comes to a hall of fame of a different sort, the **Aerospace Historical Center** housing the **International Aerospace Hall of Fame** and the **San Diego Aerospace Museum.**

The building originally served as the Palace of Transportation for the 1935 Exposition. Built in Modernist style, the circular structure is outlined by blue neon lights at night giving it the appearance of a UFO about to take off from the park. Indoors, the museum's circular walls host Juan Larrinaga's 1935 depiction of the stages in the history of transportation, the largest wall mural in North America.

The museum contains over fifty original or replica aircraft on display, including a replica of Charles

*The fountain in Balboa Park's **Plaza de Balboa** with the **Natural History Museum** in the background.*

*Three views of the **Spanish Village** art studios and boutiques in Balboa Park.*

Lindbergh's "The Spirit of St. Louis," the first plane to cross the Atlantic. Aerospace and aviation exhibits hang from the curving ceilings and walls.

A bit north of Plaza de Balboa at the eastern end of El Prado, on the way to the zoo, is the delightful **Spanish Village.**

Built in 1934-35, the village is now an art colony consisting of thirty-nine Spanish-Renaissance style cottages grouped around a colorful courtyard. The cottages house art studios and gift shops featuring painting, sculpture and ceramics. It is a pleasant, relaxed place for souvenir shopping or merely a leisurely stroll.

One of the more than thirty koalas at the **San Diego Zoo** in Balboa Park: more koalas than any other zoo in the U.S.!

*A zebra at the **San Diego Zoo**.*

On the following page:
*A giraffe and pink flamingo at the **San Diego Zoo**.*

The world-famous **San Diego Zoo** occupies a hundred acres in the north of Balboa Park. Started in 1916 with the animals left behind after the Panama-California Exposition, the zoo now receives an estimated three million visitors a year. Its wild animal collection is the largest in the world with some four thousand animals representing about eight hundred different species. Over the years the zoo has been developing nine separate ecosystems, across the park's canyons and hillsides, closely resembling the animals' natural habitats. Animals thus roam freely in barless, moated enclosures similar to their natural environments. There is an African Krall, a tropical American rain forest, and in 1991 a bioclimatic exhibit called "Gorilla Tropics" opened for lowland gorillas.

Some of the zoo's attractions which you won't want to miss are the Flamingo Lagoon, the Reptile House, the Channel Islands Sea Lion Show, the Animal Chit-Chat Show, the Sun Bear Forest, Bear Canyon, the popular koalas, Tiger River, the enormous Scripps

Aviary for rare African birds, and the Hummingbird Aviary. The Children's Zoo permits youngsters to encounter baby animals in the nursery, and touch others in the "petting paddock."

But the zoo does not limit itself to animal life. In 1991 its 128-acre tropical garden became an accredited botanical garden. In fact the zoo's outstanding botanical collection is now estimated to be worth even more than its animals!

The zoo provides transportation alternatives to those lacking the time or energy to hike the one hundred acres on foot. There are forty-minute guided open-air bus tours available. And the Skyfari Aerial Tram provides transportation 170 feet over the treetops from one end of the zoo to the other. The ride affords spectacular views of the zoo, as well as Balboa Park, the San Diego skyline, and the bay. And finally, there is a great variety of restaurants serving breakfast, snacks and lunch for those in need of nourishment during their zoo adventure.

*Three views of the **Junipero Serra Museum** in Old Town's **Presidio Park.***

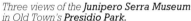

OLD TOWN'S PRESIDIO PARK

Towering over the San Diego River north of downtown is San Diego's **Presidio Park.** It was on this hilltop inland from the bay on July 16, 1769 that Spanish missionary Padre Junipero Serra and a group of soldiers led by Gaspar de Portola founded the first Catholic mission and "presidio" (fortress) in what was to become the State of California.

The Mission San Diego de Alcala was moved six miles inland in 1774 to remove the Indian converts from the mistreatment of the Spanish soldiers, and so as to be closer to the Indian villages, better agricultural land, and water sources. Today all that remains of the Spanish garrison and mission are the barest of ruins marked by mounds and depressions in the grass below the Junipero Serra Museum. A flagpole and cannon commemorate the spot where U.S. troops established Fort Stockton on the site of the original Spanish fort after the latter's capture in 1846.

Presidio Park provides a pleasant escape from the hustle and bustle of downtown San Diego. The park, landscaped with ten thousand trees and shrubs, sits high above the city. Since it is not over-visited, there is a sense of seclusion and tranquillity. There are also vast panoramas of much of San Diego County, Mission Bay and the Pacific. A favorite pastime for locals is "grass skiing" down the park's green slopes.

The park's **Junipero Serra Museum** was designed by architect William Templeton Johnson in the so-called "Mission Revival" style with red tile roofs and white stucco arches in the manner of California's historic Spanish missions.

The museum was dedicated on July 16, 1929 on the one hundred and sixtieth anniversary of Padre Serra's founding of the Mission San Diego de Alcala. Its exhibits focus on the area's Native American history, its European explorers, and the Spanish-Mexican period before San Diego became part of the U.S.

The museum's collection includes archaeological artifacts from excavations at the presidio. There are period items from the Mission and Rancho eras, and the collection of Spanish Renaissance furniture is one of the finest in the West. The museum's tower offers spectacular views.

*Views of San Diego's colorful **Old Town** district: now a State Historic Park.*

OLD TOWN

In the early 1800s, the Spanish began to settle at the base of Presidio Hill in San Diego's **Old Town** district. The six-block area just north of downtown has been a twelve-acre State Historic Park since 1968. San Diego Avenue is closed to traffic here, as is the rest of the Old Town Park area, creating an extensive pedestrian mall. Old Town is an extremely popular attraction for visitors and locals alike, due to its colorful, festive atmosphere as well as its great restaurants and small shops along tree-lined streets. In Old Town the visitor to San Diego truly comes to terms with the city's Spanish and Mexican heritages. The area is best seen on foot, and there is abundant parking available.

Old Town's center surrounds the original rectangular town plaza from the Mission era called Old Town Plaza or Plaza de las Armas. The square's central lawn is frequently the site for art shows. A flagpole marks the spot where the first U.S. flag was raised in 1846. Some of California's oldest adobe and log houses, dating from the mid-1800s, are found on the square and in the surrounding streets of Old Town.

The **Robinson-Rose House** from 1853 contains some rooms restored to their original appearance. It also houses the **Visitor's Center** where information about the park is available. There are free guided tours of Old Town as well as booklets with self-guided walking tours of the area. Horse-drawn carriages are also available.

The **Casa de Bandini** is a Spanish hacienda built in 1829 which was the city's social center during Mexican rule. It is now home to a luxurious Mexican restaurant. The **Mason Street School** is an original one-room schoolhouse. The **San Diego Union Newspaper Historical Building** is a wooden construction built in 1851 in Maine and shipped to San Diego around the tip of South America. The building housed the original *San Diego Union* newspaper offices which published the first edition of the paper in 1868. The **Seeley Stables,** San Diego's stagecoach stop after 1867, has an interesting collection of Old West memorabilia. The **Black Hawk Smithy and Stable** from the 1860s has been restored and makes for a fascinating visit. **El Campo Santo** is San Diego's original cemetery dating from 1850.

*The central courtyard with patio, and two bedrooms furnished with original period pieces, of the **Casa de Estudillo** on Old Town Plaza.*

The **Casa de Estudillo** on Old Town Plaza was one of the social and political centers of San Diego during the Mexican and early American periods. The retired commander of the presidio, Capitan Jose Maria Estudillo, began construction of the house in 1829 and it continued until the 1850s. The two-story wood and adobe structure was built mainly with the labor of the local Kumeyaay Indians. It was restored in 1908 and 1968, and is now a museum of the Estudillo family cattle ranchers. The rooms are furnished with original period pieces similar to those in the house before 1860.

Old Town's most popular attraction is without doubt the **Bazaar del Mundo.** Constructed in 1971, the Bazaar receives over four million visitors annually. A central Mexican-style courtyard is surrounded by sixteen brightly colored boutiques and four restaurants. The original 1824 wood and adobe childhood home of Governor Pio Pico with its eight entrances is now a centerpiece of the Bazaar as well as a popular restaurant. The courtyard is planted with brilliant flowers, and is the site of frequent arts and crafts shows, and Mexican festivals. On weekends the gazebo hosts folkloric dancers.

Heritage Park on a slope along the eastern edge of Old Town is a 7.8-acre park with cobblestone sidewalks created to save many of San Diego's fine old Victorian houses from destruction. Landmark buildings in danger of demolition in other parts of the city have been carefully moved to Heritage Park, and then restored. They now house shops, offices, bed and breakfasts, and restaurants. Among the park's rescued buildings are the **Temple Beth Israel,** the first synagogue in Southern California, the **Sherman-Gilbert House** (1887), the **Bushyhead House** (1887), and the **Christian House** (1889).

*The facade, interior, and courtyard of the **Mission San Diego de Alcala** in San Diego's Mission Valley.*

THE MISSION SAN DIEGO DE ALCALA

California's first Catholic church and mission, the **Mission San Diego de Alcala,** was consecrated by the Spanish Franciscan missionary Padre Junipero Serra within the walls of the Spanish garrison at the top of Presidio Hill on July 16, 1769. But problems soon arose between the Mission's Indian converts and the abusive Spanish soldiers stationed at the presidio. There were also problems with water supplies, and the land along the slopes of Presidio Hill was not especially suited for agriculture. So in 1774 Padre Serra moved the Mission to its present location six miles inland in Mission Valley along the San Diego River. Here the Mission was closer to the local Indian villages, and the Native Americans were spared the soldiers' mistreatment and harassment. The land also proved better for farming and there was greater access to water sources.

The Franciscan Missionaries aggressively worked to convert the indigenous population to Roman Catholicism. European farming methods were introduced and the Indians were increasingly forced

to abandon their semi-nomadic lifestyles in order to provide their labor to the Mission enterprise.

Resistance was not long in coming, and in 1775 the Mission was attacked and burned to the ground. Padre Luis Jayme was killed in the attack, and thus came to be considered California's first Catholic martyr. The other Mission occupants managed to escape to the fort on Presidio Hill.

But the Spanish persisted in their colonial project, and in 1776 Padre Serra began reconstruction of the San Diego Mission. This time the missionaries covered the walls with adobe and used tile roofs to make the buildings virtually fire resistant. By 1780 most of the buildings had been completed in the typical Spanish Mission-style architecture of thick adobe walls with red tile roofs and white stucco arches in a quadrangle around a central courtyard and patio where people could gather. The church itself is rather simple and unpretentious in style. Padre Jayme is buried in the Mission sanctuary.

The San Diego Mission was the first in a long chain of twenty-one missions, each a day's journey apart,

along California's El Camino Real ("royal highway") going north along the California coast. San Diego's Mission was known as "the Mother of the Missions." By 1800 about 1,500 Native Americans had been baptized and were living and working on the Mission grounds. Indian labor was used to plant 50,000 acres with beans, corn, wheat and barley. Vineyards, orchards and vegetable gardens were planted around the Mission. Livestock included 20,000 sheep, 10,000 cattle, and 1,250 horses.

When Mexico won its independence from Spain in 1821, the Franciscan missionaries refused their allegiance to the revolutionary Mexican regime, and returned to Spain. The Mexican government then secularized the California Missions, and the lands of the Mission San Diego de Alcala were given to Santiago Arguello.

The Mission was then occupied by the U.S. Cavalry from the outbreak of the U.S. war against Mexico in 1846 until the Mission's lands were given back to the Catholic Church by U.S. President Abraham Lincoln in 1862. Pope Paul VI declared the Mission a minor basilica in 1976.

An aerial view of the world-famous **Hotel del Coronado** with tennis courts, swimming pool and the stupendous Coronado Beach in the foreground, Glorietta Bay, the San Diego-Coronado Bay Bridge and the San Diego skyline in the background.

CORONADO

South of downtown across the San Diego Bay is the island-like community of **Coronado.** Although seeming to have the appearance and atmosphere of an island, virtually surrounded by the waters of the bay and the Pacific Ocean, Coronado is actually at the northern end of a peninsula connected to the mainland by a highway over a long, narrow sand spit called the **Silver Strand.**
In 1932 the **Silver Strand State Beach** was created, a popular place for clam digging and surf fishing.

Since 1969 Coronado may be reached from downtown by the **San Diego-Coronado Bay Bridge.** The bridge is an architectural wonder, curving 2.2 miles across the bay and soaring 246 feet above the water at its highest point.

The trip across the bridge affords a splendid view of the bay, Coronado, and the San Diego skyline.

Another pleasant way to reach Coronado is with the convenient **Bay Ferry** running the distance between the B Street Pier at downtown's Embarcadero and Coronado's Old Ferry Landing in a mere five minutes. The Old Ferry Landing in Coronado has been transformed into a delightful dining and shopping center with many small boutiques and fine restaurants. There are great views of the harbor and the city skyline from benches along the waterfront, and bicycles may be rented for touring Coronado's wide streets.

Coronado itself is a peaceful community of about 25,000 with its own city government. Large Victorian houses line quiet tree-lined streets, and there are eighteen or so public parks. Coronado has twenty-eight miles of superb sandy beaches. There is a truly island-like atmosphere about the place. Residents refer to Coronado as "the village."

In the center of town is the 8-acre **Spreckels Park**. The park is a favorite spot for weekend kite-flying and picnics, Sunday art shows, and concerts at the bandstand in the summer.
Among the city's eighty-six registered historic homes and sites is the Meade House (1896) where L. Frank Baum wrote *The Wizard of Oz*.

Other buildings worthy of note are the 1898 Stephens-Terry House, the 1894 Coronado Victorian House, the 1901 Jessop House, the 1909 Coronado Library, the 1890 Graham Memorial Presbyterian Church, the 1894 Christ Episcopal Church, the 1920 Sacred Heart Church, the 1887 Baby Del, the 1908 Claus Spreckels House, the 1901 Crown Manor, and the 1899 Mary Cossitt House.

The Coronado Visitors Information Center at 1111 Orange Avenue will provide all the brochures, guides and other information necessary to visit the town. Guided tours are also available.

Coronado's most famous monument is the incredible **Hotel del Coronado,** a State Historical Landmark since 1977.
Hotel founder Elisha Babcock had the dream of building a hotel that "would be the talk of the Western World."

The result was a Victorian masterpiece built in one year through the labors of hundreds of Chinese construction workers.

Completed in 1888, the resort hotel is world-famous for its wooden, ginger-bread architecture with cupolas, gables, window peaks, and red roofs. The world's first electrically lighted hotel, it was inaugurated by Thomas Edison.

The hotel's 399 rooms overlooking the Pacific and its fine beaches have been popular throughout the years with visiting politicians, celebrities, royalty and dignitaries. Twelve U.S. presidents have been

*The incredible **San Diego-Coronado Bay Bridge** curving 2.2 miles across San Diego Bay from downtown to Coronado.*

*An aerial view of **Coronado Island** with the **Hotel del Coronado** and the dome of its Crown Room: an unsupported 33-foot-high dome of handfitted sugar pine with no nails!*

*A view of the **Hotel del Coronado** from beautiful Coronado Beach.*

entertained there as guests.

The hotel's evocative setting has also provided the location for films such as Billy Wilder's 1958 comedy *Some Like it Hot* with Marilyn Monroe, Tony Curtis and Jack Lemmon, and *The Stuntman* with Peter O'Toole in 1980.

A 7-story tower with three hundred modern rooms and the Grand Hotel with a 1,500 person capacity were added after the 1960s.

The Hotel del Coronado now has seven hundred rooms. There are tennis courts, a gazebo in the garden, a swimming pool, boutiques, galleries, two bars and three restaurants. The Crown Room Restaurant is particularly impressive, with an

unsupported 33-foot high domed ceiling of sugar pine hand-fitted without a single nail. The room's chandeliers were designed by *Wizard of Oz* author L. Frank Baum. Plan on spending several hours wandering around the premises in order to get a feel for the grandeur of the place. For a glimpse at the colorful details of the hotel's, and Coronado's, historic background, the Historical Gallery is well worth a visit.

Aviation pioneer Glenn Curtis established the first flying school in the U.S. on North Island at the northern end of the Coronado peninsula in 1910. The site was also the point of departure for Charles Lindbergh's flight around the world. North Island became home to the U.S. Naval Air Station in 1917.

A view of San Diego Harbor with the marinas of man-made
Shelter Island in the foreground, and **Harbor Island**
in the background on the left.

Harbor And Shelter Island

Harbor Island is a man-made island in the San
Diego Harbor. It was constructed from three and a
half million tons of rock and earth dredged from the
San Diego Bay to allow access to Navy aircraft
carriers. The island is connected to the downtown
mainland, not far from the San Diego International
Airport, by a strip of land.

To the east is **Shelter Island**, another island-
peninsula built with the earth dredged from the bay.
Both are lined with marinas, shipyards, hotels, and
restaurants.

There are many sportfishing party boats, diving
charters, and whale-watching boats which leave
from the area.

Parks and picturesque walkways line the waterfront,
and there are always wonderful views of the bay.

Mission Bay

North of San Diego on the coast between Point Loma
and La Jolla is the **Mission Bay Aquatic Park**.
The area was an enormous tidal swamp until the
1960s, when it was dredged to form a man-made
bay. Twenty-five million cubic yards of mud and
stone were removed in all.
The resulting acquatic park is a virtual paradise for
water sports and recreation: sailing, water-skiing,
windsurfing, fishing, swimming, kite flying, jogging,
cycling, picnicking, golfing, tennis, volleyball,
camping, and more!

The park covers 4,600 acres of which seventy-five
per cent is public land. There are twenty-seven
miles of bayfront beaches, seventeen miles of
oceanfront, and acres of green lawns.
Docking is available for 2,500 boats.
Marina Bay has resort hotels, marinas, restaurants,
and amusement centers, all constructed with respect

for the park's natural environment.

Mission Beach, one of San Diego's most popular, is a two-mile stretch of white sandy beach on a narrow peninsula between Mission Bay and the Pacific. This is the Southern California beach scene at its most wild and crazy! Surfing championships are held here annually. A three-mile boardwalk runs from Belmont Park to Pacific Beach.

SEA WORLD

Opened on the shores of Mission Bay in 1964, **Sea World** attracts an estimated three and a half million visitors each year. Covering one hundred and fifty acres, it is the world's largest marine-life park. There are ninety-minute guided tours to allow visitors to get their bearings, as well as a glimpse behind the scenes.

Sea World's 320-foot Skytower offers visitors a glass-elevator ride to its summit from which much of San Diego County may be seen.

*A scene from the killer whale show at **Shamu Stadium**.*

*The 5-million gallon **Shamu Stadium** where Shamu the 3-ton killer whale and his companions Baby Shamu, Namu and Nakina perform acrobatic feats for the public*

Among the major attractions are Shamu the three-ton killer whale and his companions Baby Shamu, Namu and Nakina. They perform in the five million gallon Shamu Stadium, leaping as high as twenty-four feet out of the water and thoroughly soaking the public in the front rows with their acrobatic antics! The 300-square foot "Shamuvision" television screen allows the public to follow all moments of the show, close-up.

Another major attraction is the Penguin Encounter with its moving sidewalk which takes visitors past a glass-enclosed polar habitat with more than three hundred Emperor Penguins from the Antarctic. At the walrus, seal and sea lion exhibits it is possible to feed the animals. The Shark Encounter is the largest of its kind in the world, with an aquarium which includes a 9-foot, 450-lb. lemon shark. The dolphin and whale show is also fascinating.

The Wings of the World Exhibition is the largest bird of prey show in the world with seventy-five performing birds from six continents. At the California Tidal Pool Exhibition, children can touch sea urchins, star fish and other shore life. There are also sea turtles, Alaska sea otters, a freshwater aquarium with piranhas, and marine aquariums with bat rays and moray eels. The Cap'n Kid's World provides extensive playground facilities for the children. The glass-elevator ride to the top of the 320-foot Skytower offers spectacular panoramas of much of San Diego County. On summer nights from June through September 15, Sea World hosts live concerts and fireworks shows.

The statue of Portuguese explorer Juan Rodriguez Cabrillo at the **Cabrillo National Monument** *on the tip of the Point Loma peninsula.*

The original 1854 **Point Loma Lighthouse.**

POINT LOMA

Point Loma is a peninsula of exceptional natural beauty curving around the mouth of the San Diego Bay to the west of Coronado. Its rugged cliffs tower as high as five hundred and fifty feet over the Pacific. The peninsula protects San Diego's bay and downtown from the tides and storms of the Pacific Ocean.

The **Fort Rosecrans National Cemetery** with its 71-acre garden and 47,000 white tombstones marking the graves of San Diego's fallen soldiers offers a unique setting for panoramic visions of the bay and ocean.

On Point Loma's southern tip is the **Cabrillo National Monument,** established in 1913 in honor of the Portuguese explorer Juan Rodriguez Cabrillo who landed at Point Loma on September 28, 1542. The monument covers one hundred forty-four acres of wind-swept pines and junipers. Portuguese sculptor Alvario de Bree's original 1904 statue was replaced by a new statue in 1989.

The **Visitor Center** has a good book and gift shop, and provides information about the park, including daily films and lectures in the auditorium. There are also exhibits on Cabrillo's voyage. The panoramic views include the San Bernardino Mountains two hundred miles to the northeast, the hills around Tijuana to the south, as well as the Pacific Ocean and San Diego Bay. On the east side of the point is the

Bayside Trail for hikers, winding down and along the steep rocky slopes past the hunting grounds of the Digueno Indians. On the western coast of the point are tidal pools which can be explored at low tide. They contain a hundred different species of plants and animals, including flowering anemones, crustaceans, starfish and octupus.

The **Point Loma Lighthouse** was constructed on top of Point Loma in 1854. The white sandstone structure is open to visitors. It is four hundred twenty-two feet above sea level, overlooking the ocean and the bay, and was meant to serve both as a coastal beacon and a harbor light. In clear weather the light was visible for twenty-five miles, but low clouds and fog often obscured it, causing it to be replaced by a Coast Guard Lighthouse on the water's edge at the bottom of the hill in 1891.

The **Whale Overlook** at the tip of Point Loma is the ideal place to view the annual gray whale migration. From mid-December till the end of February, the gray whales pass Point Loma on their 6,000-mile migration from their summer feeding grounds in the Bering Sea to the warm shallow lagoons of Baja California, where they give birth. The whales travel in "pods" of three to five, close to the coastline. Weighing up to forty tons and measuring up to fifty feet long, the whales make a spectacular sight as they swim along jumping up to thirty feet out of the water. There are only an estimated 17,000 California Gray whales in existence today.

LA JOLLA

North of Mission Beach is the exclusive coastal community of **La Jolla**. Officially part of San Diego, La Jolla has a small-town atmosphere. Its wide boulevards are lined with eucalyptus, palms and cedar, and expensive houses worth millions. The town center is called "the Village," and is an exclusive dining and shopping center with expensive boutiques, antique dealers, jewelry stores, art galleries, import shops and gourmet restaurants.

La Jolla is also known as "the Jewel of the Pacific," with its seven miles of spectacular coastline including some of the best surfing beaches in San Diego. The sixties surfers of Windansea Beach were immortalized in Tom Wolfe's *The Pumphouse Gang.* La Jolla Cove is an exceptional attraction with its sandstone cliffs, caves, towering palms, and excellent snorkelling. Further south is the Children's Pool, whose shallow waters make it ideal for families and young snorkellers. On the cliffs above the shore is the beautifully-landscaped Scripps Park where one can stroll along taking in the splendor of the coast and the sublime sunsets over the Pacific.

The University of California at San Diego is spread across 1,200 acres on the bluffs overlooking La Jolla. Famous for its award-winning architecture, UCSD is one of the top ten research universities in the nation. The university's Scripps Institute of Oceanography is one of the largest in the world. La Jolla is also home to the Scripps Clinic and Research Foundation, and the Salk Institute. The San Diego Museum of Contemporary Art is located in a building which dates from 1916 but has been added on to over the years. The Stephen Birch Aquarium-Museum with its thirty-six aquariums and outdoor tidal pool replaced the Scripps Aquarium in 1992.

The Torrey Pines State Reserve on 1,700 acres of rugged terrain along the north coast of La Jolla is home to the extremely rare Torrey pine tree. The Torrey Pines Beach is one of the finest in the entire county. And there is no better way to end a day at the beach than by watching the magnificent colors of the sunset over the Pacific from the groves of twisted Torrey pines atop the three hundred foot sandstone cliffs towering over the pounding surf below.

A bird's-eye view of **La Jolla's** *rugged coast.*

A sheltered cove and white sandy beach in **La Jolla.**

Pelicans rest on rocks along the shore's edge at **La Jolla.**

A field of brilliantly colored ranunculus arranged in horizontal stripes.

*Focus on a few **Giant Tecelote® Ranunculus** blooms.*

THE FLOWER FIELDS ®

From March through April, fifty-plus acres of fields explode in bright colors with ranunculus flowers on a hillside at **Flower Fields** at **Carlsbad Ranch**. Every spring, for more than thirty years, the pretty community of Carlsbad, 30 miles from downtown San Diego (a 45-min. drive), has provided a display of the region's most beautiful flowers.

Dry summers, mild winters and well-drained sandy soil are what really makes this presentation such a spectacular sight, which can be even more striking at its peak with over eight million ranunculus blossoms overlooking the Pacific Ocean. Essentially the flowers are grown for their bulbs and only few of them are sold. The Flower Fields is the only working farm allowing the public to tiptoe through its fields and also one of the largest **Giant Tecelote® Ranunculus** bulb production operations in the world.

LEGOLAND® California

LEGOLAND California is the first theme park built in the United States by the Danish toy-maker. The 128-acre site includes 5,000 models created from 30 million LEGO® bricks, 40 rides and attractions to be 'kid's powered'.

LEGOLAND adventure starts at **The Beginning** and develops into six major themed "blocks": **Village Green**, created with large DUPLO® bricks and a huge Playtown - **Fun Town**, site of the pint-size driving school - **Castle Hill**, an enchanted medieval setting - **The Ridge**, where visitors take a self-propelled ride to the top of a tower and "free-fall" to the bottom - **The Lake**, featuring passenger boats for lakeshore and Miniland tours - Miniland, a 1:20 scale reproduction of American landmarks - **The Imagination Zone**, a learning center equipped with computers utilizing the LEGO software.

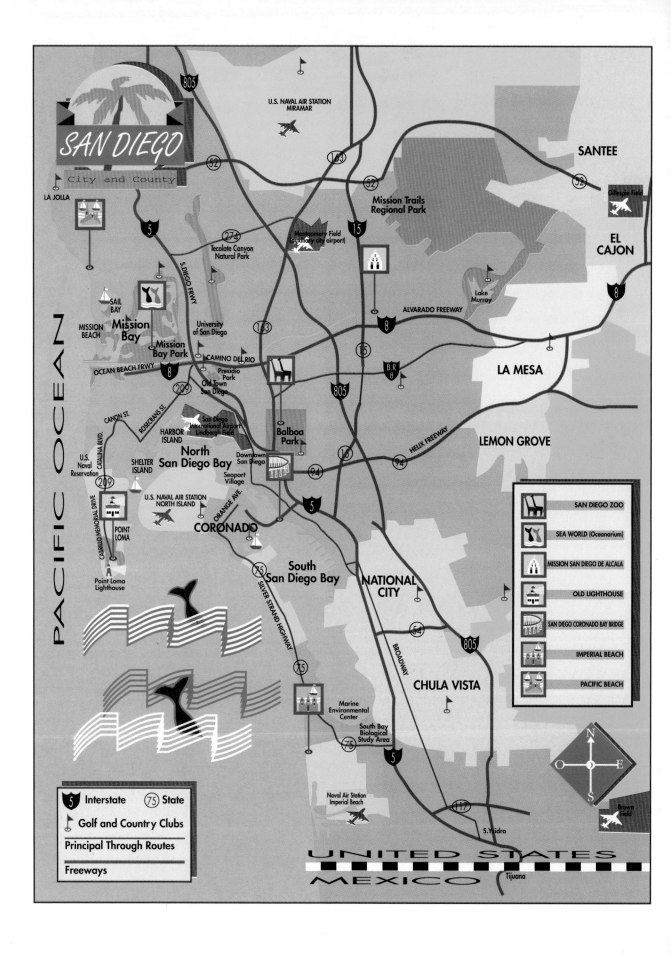